*McGraw-Hill Higher Education*

*A Division of The **McGraw-Hill** Companies*

SERVICES MARKETING: INTEGRATING CUSTOMER FOCUS ACROSS THE FIRM
Published by McGraw-Hill/Irwin, a business unit of The McGraw-Hill Companies, Inc., 1221 Avenue of the Americas, New York, NY, 10020. Copyright © 2003, 2000, 1996 by The McGraw-Hill Companies, Inc. All rights reserved. No part of this publication may be reproduced or distributed in any form or by any means, or stored in a database or retrieval system, without the prior written consent of The McGraw-Hill Companies, Inc.., including, but not limited to, in any network or other electronic storage or transmission, or broadcast for distance learning.
Some ancillaires, including electronic and print components, may not be available to customers outside the United States.

This book is printed on acid-free paper.

domestic        2 3 4 5 6 7 8 9 0 CCW/CCW 0 9 8 7 6 5 4 3 2
international    2 3 4 5 6 7 8 9 0 CCW/CCW 0 9 8 7 6 5 4 3 2

ISBN 0-07-247142-5

Publisher:   *John E. Biernat*
Executive editor:   *Gary L. Bauer*
Developmental editor:   *Scott Becker*
Marketing manager:   *Kim Kanakes*
Producer, media technology:   *Todd Labak*
Project manager:   *Destiny Rynne*
Senior production supervisor:   *Michael R. McCormick*
Coordinator freelance design:   *Artemio Ortiz, Jr.*
Photo research coordinator:   *Jeremy Cheshareck*
Photo researcher:   *Jennifer Blankenship*
Supplemt producer:   *Betty Hadala*
Cover design:   *Trudi Gershenov*
Typeface:   *10.5/12 New Times Roman*
Compositor:   *ElectraGraphics, Inc.*
Printer:   *Courier/Westford*

**Library of Congress Cataloging-in-Publication Data**

Zeithaml, Valarie A.
    Services marketing: integrating customer focus across the firm / Valarie A. Zeithaml,
Mary Jo Bitner.—3rd ed.
        p.  cm.
    Includes index.
    ISBN 0-07-247142-5 (alk. paper)—ISBN 0-07-119914-4 (international ed.: alk. paper)
    1. Service industries—Marketing.  2. Customer services.  3. Marketing.  I. Bitner, Mary
Jo.  II. Title.
HD9980.5 .Z45  2003
658.8—dc21                                          20020255 44

INTERNATIONAL EDITION ISBN 0-07-119914-4
Copyright © 2003. Exclusive rights by The McGraw-Hill Companies, Inc. for manufacture and export.
This book cannot be re-exported from the country to which it is sold by McGraw-Hill.
The International Edition is not available in North America.

www.mhhe.com

# SERVICES MARKETING

**Integrating Customer Focus
Across the Firm**

Third Edition

**Valarie A. Zeithaml**
*University of North Carolina*

**Mary Jo Bitner**
*Arizona State University*

Boston   Burr Ridge, IL   Dubuque, IA   Madison, WI   New York   San Francisco   St. Loui
Bangkok   Bogotá   Caracas   Kuala Lumpur   Lisbon   London   Madrid   Mexico City
Milan   Montreal   New Delhi   Santiago   Seoul   Singapore   Sydney   Taipei   Toronto